LOOKING FOR
A SOFT PLACE
TO LAND

Looking for a Soft Place to Land

poems by
cin salach

TIA CHUCHA PRESS
CHICAGO

ACKNOWLEDGMENTS

"You Have the Right Not to Remain Silent" and "Open Mouths" were first published in *Hammers* Magazine. Thanks, Nat.

Thanks to the Marx—Messing, Smith, and Penner-Howell. Thanks to the Goddesses—Paula, Sheila, Lisa, Marcia, Donna, Pat and Madelaine. Thanks to Morgan, Mary, Jenny and Beau, the ritual meal group, the women at Irene's Place, Kurt, Michael, Luis, Brigid, Seth, Max and the never-ceases-to-amaze-me poetry community found and found again in Chi-town.

Printed in the United States of America.

ISBN 1-882688-11-2
Library of Congress Catalog Card Number: 96-60119

Book Design: Jane Brunette
Front Cover Design and Illustration: Mark Penner-Howell
Back Cover Photo: Jeanine Deubel

PUBLISHED BY:
TIA CHUCHA
PRESS
A *Project of the*
Guild Complex
PO Box 476969
Chicago, IL 60647

DISTRIBUTED BY:
NORTHWESTERN
UNIVERSITY PRESS
Chicago Distribution
Center
11030 S. Langley
Chicago, IL 60628

Funding for this project was partially provided by the National Endowment for the Arts, the Illinois Arts Council, and the Lannan Foundation.

In memory of Donis

Table of Contents

FREEING THE FOSSIL

It is the language of words
and it is unlike anything
I have heard
with my fingers.
They are forming sounds
and in their stillness,
their eagerness shines
wide open and spilling
over everything
that is white or anything
that has been left alone too long.

They are telling me to dream
in colors I have not yet dreamed
and now
they are building me a house
to raise you in.
I had no idea they could be this gentle.
Their persistent prickling,
the stiff feathers that make my bed
so enduring.
They go on and on

and I wonder if they know me,
if they know where they are taking me,
and if they have been there before.

Together, we step carefully
through the unfinished bodies.
Translucent carcasses hold us in place
and eyes, or what once was,
stare up at me.
Memory, though I don't know whose,
makes them glisten with some kind of emotion
I have not yet touched.

Their stories have fertilized this ground
where the next step waits to fall,
and I raise to my lips this floor
of history's forest.
I lift it up to my mouth,
but before it can touch my tongue
for swallowing,
it sprouts wings.
It becomes the sky.

You Have the Right
Not to Remain Silent

I could throw my arms
in the air and say
I had nothing to do with it,
I wasn't there.
I was there, but I wasn't looking.
I was looking, but I wasn't seeing.
I was seeing, but I wasn't caring.

I could throw my arms
in the air and say
What's the point?
Nothing that dull can ever be
sharpened, really.
Nothing that sharp can ever be
softened, really.

I could throw my arms
in the air and say
Just lay me back down to sleep, please.
It's six a.m. in Chi-town
and I am dreaming of you.

It's six a.m. in Moscow
and I am dreaming of you.
It's six a.m. in Berlin,
and a wall comes tumbling down.
Pieces of rock are marketable here.
Signs of life have become scarce.
While a flag of every color
flies over history, blowing
its ancient lesson across the land:
Silence is not golden.
Not here. Not ever.
Peace is not a quiet thing.
Do not let them hold your tongue.

And it's six a.m. in Prague
and the dream has been woken.
Whispers wind their way through the square,
push at people's backs,
blow across their hearts,
tell them to speak up:
Freedom for all! Freedom for all!

And somewhere a world
starts over from the top.
Determined to get it right
this time, to play fair.
To never let things
get this way again.

And somewhere peace begins
to pound in someone's heart.
Make its way up the throat.
Into the mouth.
To become a voice.
For someone to hear.
And another to translate,
and another to act on,
and another to live for,
and another to die for,

and I could throw my arms
in the air and let them
fall around you.
Hold you.
Know you.
Whisper *peace*.
Scream it out loud.
Because silence is not golden.
Not here, not ever.

VELVET

for Vaclav Havel

I can't tell you much, except
for the graceful aging,
the strength of history,
how young and hungry this city let me be.
If you don't know the language, you must
let your heart do all the talking.
If you don't know the language, it's easier
to believe what you hear.

I can't tell you much, except
how I cried the first time
I walked across the Charles Bridge.
The weight of it under my feet
lifting me up like a child
able to see it all in one breath.
My lungs filling with every
ancient hero, and the castle,
and the river thick and strong,
and the little old men fishing
or not fishing and the music,
gypsy born, teasing
the bottoms of my soul,

asking me to dance and
not taking no for an answer.
How all my definitions for beautiful
started scrambling for better words
in my head, and my American mouth,
awe-shaped and eager,
let the gulls fly in and out
searching for bits of bread
to fill their own.

I can't tell you much, except
how freedom felt here.
Frenzied and fresh,
newborn and nearly disastrous.
So much future to never regret again,
and every day a fantastic gift
from God, or someone
in an equally exalted position.

I can't tell you much, except
how the memory of revolution
hangs in the air like velvet.
And in every spot where
the absence of bullets made peace
scream through this city like fire,
the first furious flames burn bright
on their way to the green and
golden era of spring.

GET HUMAN

This is what we do best:
Hurt each other.
Pushing and pulling
until flesh fades to black, blue.

The border between love and hate
is a canyon of thin lines
crossed again and again.
You want to believe your body
is not conditioned for this until,
swallowing whole skyfuls of air,
you remember your own birth.
The slow process of surfacing.
The cutting of the cord.
The first thin line, crossed.

This is what we do best:
Say good-bye before
the wet wording of hello
has even had time to dry.
Now the border is a single breath,

a gesture, a thought
on the tip of your tongue
gone before you could speak it.
It is awkward to think of love
and hate so close
they could almost touch.

Now the border is you.

WITH YOU

written with Sheila Donohue

With you
I made up all the questions
so you could have all the answers.

With you I left the lights on
so I could watch you, slowly,
one by one by all,
break day into night.

I locked hundreds of doors
and left my map at home
to see where you would lead me.
To see the priority of moments you intended
with me holding your hand
and you holding my breath.

And the last thing I recall . . .
I was dancing on a rooftop,
sending my echo down a mountaintop,
starfish reeling me down to sea level.

The last thing . . .
I was walking barefoot
on the sandy bottom of the world
looking for necessary treasure, fleshy fins
and all that oxygen dripping into the salty sea.

I was shedding sky, breathing oceans.
I was racing dolphins.
I was kissing the moon goodbye.
And as I surfaced near the beginning
as you let go of earth's anchor

I was knee deep in the muddy center of the world
seconds away from your garden.

We gazed over God's ravine.
You rubbed mint leaves into the curves of my back.
And with each step forward
we talked to strange species.

High flying hawks conversed with the wind.

CHURCH

We sit in the belly of God
hearts growling, organs twisting,
mouths folded in prayer.
We know the sky is waiting
beyond these ribs, divine.
Ribs that promise to crack wide
every seventh day.
Digestion resting,
God remembering
our appetite for living, sin.

We sit in the belly of God
backs bent straight
for confession.
Tongues resting
on windows, waiting
for wine and Sunday
is just past our reach.

Hearts growling,
organs twisting,

bones begin to rattle,
drawing attention to our flesh
which is burning, our soul
which is barely visible.
We are hallucinating
Forgiveness.
We are hallucinating
wine and Sunday
is just past our reach.

We know the sky is waiting
beyond these ribs, divine.
Our mouths, circled
in offering, exhale
Exultation.
Filling the river
where we'll swim, full of fish,
upwards, bare.
Hearty and heartened.

Sunday, just past.

GOING HOME

It was every word in between
what had been written
and what was left to write:
A million pages, unsung alphabets
nursery rhymes stillborn at the age of fourteen.

I got that feeling
life is never as simple as this
and death is harder still, when
the dying thing is coveting
your breath, as well.

You can visit me here, but this ain't my home.
You can send letters postcards pictures here
but this ain't my home.
You may know me by name
but that was only luck
and yes, this ain't my home.
I am generous with my secrets, though,
and you sure look like you could use one
so I'll let you in on this: At night, see,
when the doors are locked

and everyone has left, the world
comes to me for a place to stay.
And then I am home.
My body a building scraping the sky.
It is that tall! Rooms for all . . .
running water and loaves of sweet bread.
We sit around my heart. A warm fire
crackles there and I feed history
with stories of my life until fat and sleepy
it closes its eyes to dream of tomorrow.

Memory is a hungry thing, I know.
Feed it once and it will keep coming back
to you, but ain't that what home is for?
I know. And I know that
when morning comes it will leave me here.
Night is a child, but Day is a
full grown answer to dreaming

make it happen while the sun shines girl

and I cannot find room in my house
for that much sunshine.
So when morning comes
and knocks at my heart
the fire is cold.
I am already gone.
There ain't nobody home.
No body. No home.

MORE

Her fingers are not new
to this pushing and polishing
rough into smooth.
Nothing into something.
Something into more.

Her fingers have found a way
to shape what was once horror
into the place she now calls home.

Every secret sculpted deep into that clay
is a breath taken and held
until it becomes something
in the right light
at the right moment
once or twice a day.

Every day
her elbows are up to here
in secrets
that must be shaped and reshaped
and reshaped until suddenly (not really)

they are something
in the right light.
Or the wrong light.
Or they become the light
hot white and burning until
suddenly (really)
they go dark.

And her fingers
and her elbows
and her secrets
begin again.
Pushing and polishing
rough into smooth.
Nothing
into something.
Something
into more.

THE CHEATED HEART

You bleed slowly
and deep.
Stand still while years of
horror spill out
from these veins
tapped and torn,
from this muscle
muted and mutilated.
You do not remove the pointed arrow
from your heart
for fear the hole it leaves will be too big
to ever fill back in.
For fear the hole it leaves will only
invite more of the same:
Holes. And hole makers.
Suddenly drawn to you like a magnet.
As if your heart
was made of metal.
And could never have bled so well
in the first place.

WIND DRUNK WOMEN

Wind drunk
women may leave
most men to cry
over raw pink
skies and lazy gardens,
but like the moon,
they must do their
dreaming by day
and sleep when
no one is watching.

BETTY'S MOUTH

There was a hole in you
where all your words
slipped through
and I tried not to look.
I didn't want to see your next thoughts.
I didn't want to know your next line.
I didn't want to claim your tongue
as mine, but
there was a hole in you
where all your words
slipped through.
You
couldn't understand why you kept running out
but I knew.
I tried to stuff them back into you
and they stuck to me like glue.
It hardly seemed fair.
It hardly seemed true.
But there was a hole in you
where all your words
slipped through.

BLONDE

for Marilyn

She found it was the blondeness
that was the hardest to smile through.
The bleached-to-blatant innocence
glamour-puss-platinum-pucker-up-and-here-I-come-baby
Hollywood Hair
that turned his head
                 her stomach
the most.
Happy Birthday to you . . .
Well, until that.

It was the way she, Jackie B., was so completely
Brunette.
It was the bra size, the lip shade
the skirt blowing up over the dirty breeze
of an underground train
and the breathy way the world responded
that broke his back
                 her heart
the most.

Whose hair is this on your jacket, Jack?
Well, until that.

Boobs, brains, talent, future
every one a false front
when she, Jackie B., was so real.

(The hair was flipped,
the jacket was pink,
the brains were blown,
the heart was flattened
and flattened
and finally
flattened.)

It was the funeral, the fuss, the fame
that followed her now, hounded her now,
twenty-four hours a day, a lifetime.
Her kids, their story, his affairs, her careers
whatever blows your skirt up, world
and it seemed to be her, now.
She was the dirty breeze,
the other hair on the jacket.
And who would have thought
they'd have something in common
after all these years.

Not John, boy.
Maybe Einstein.
Maybe he knew all along.

THE NIGHT I MARRIED
MY TELEVISION SET

It was the blue light running through my veins
that started my heart again.
The flickering pulse of an emotional script
that made me forget my blue promise.
It was the tunnel of electricity
that shot me forward into you.
Into tomorrow.
Into one moment on instant replay
instantly replaying me into you
forever.

It was more than a radio could ever dream of being.

It was me sucking on sound waves
crashing against the screen.
It was the midnight preacher man
seducing me into the star-spangled banner
before the world dawned
before tomorrow woke.
It was that midnight man
blessing me through you

using your voice
finding my bluest vein
and tying hard knots.
It was the scream
that never came
that finally convinced me
it was you. Muted.
And me
mouthing the words.

I'm a Stranger Here, Myself

My body
has
different ages.
Each muscle
its own personality.
Each curve
a mood.
It is no wonder morning finds me   confused.

Each part of my body prefers
a different kind of music.
When I walk
a chorus
accompanies
my footsteps.
It is no wonder I have a hard time
stopping
once I start moving.

In the stillness of privacy
privacy changes meaning
from my brain to my belly.

From my tongue to my toes.
My thighs
have actually gone so far as to build
a single-family home
around the most female part of my person

ality.
It is no wonder intimacy finds me   alone.

Each part of my body has different ideas about
where it should go.
And how it should look
upon arrival.
Putting one foot in front of the other
is more likely to cause
chaos
than forward movement.

This should result in slow motion
or chronic stillness.
And more often than not
moments happen by me
blurred.

Because of this
I have learned to take the long way
all the way
around.

It is no wonder.

OPEN MOUTHS

In my dream I was wishing
I had another language
to speak to you in.
We could wrap black
and yellow tongues
around white lips
and kiss all night long.

In my dream I was talking to you.
Thank you was the language
we spoke, the reason
our lips moved to sound.
Thank you was everything
we had to say.
Everything we needed
to kneel and love,
hold and heal.
In my dream, our new
language was hot
and sharp and brilliant
and blue.
Clear blue,

cloudless.
Thank you
was the language
we spoke, and

when the sun spoke
we held our hands
to our mouths
filling ourselves
on prayer.
Such a meal
we never knew.
And *bless you*
was the language
we heard.

BIRTH DAYS

for Mom

She wonders
if it will always be this hard
knowing Home
from any other place she went to visit
and then wanted to stay.
She wonders if her fear of fences
isn't something she made up
so she wouldn't have to fly
without excuses.
She dreams of going fast.
Of giving birth to an arrow.
Of always knowing the one direction
that will get her there without stopping even once
for coffee, or conversation.
She wonders about the second she was born.
If anyone recognized her
without a name, or hair.
If maybe she should have phoned first
instead of screaming head first
already late for the world
It's me! I made it! I'm here!

Light the first candle
and let's get on with it already . . .

She wonders what she was thinking
the moment before that heartbeat
became her own and would it always
beat this loud at beginnings?
She wanted a promise that it would.
She wanted to know that one thing for sure.
She could be happy leaving the rest to fate
if the wonder of beginnings would beat
this loud and this strong in her
every time.
She dreams about a room before
this one and wonders how she
can ever say *thank you,* or *good-bye.*

She writes *I love you* 388,800 times.
Once for every second she spent
in the warm holding pattern
that rocked her from August to April.
The rhythm of womb
that taught her to dance
and then sang her to sleep.
She wonders how nine months would look
with lots of frosting and candles.
If her mother even felt like eating cake
at this particular moment, or

who could cut a slice big enough?

FIBERS OF ME

for Dad

You were my first smile
my first name
my first prince.
But I was born
outside of you
away from you
because of you
I am the child
rushing for a reason
to every question
never asked.
Sometimes I feel like your stray thread.
Someone tugs
and I unravel
and you don't
look the same.
Most times I revel
in these beautiful clothes
you gave me at birth.
I like how they fit
no one else but me.

There are times
I believe they are
much too big, but you
just laugh and whisper
"you'll grow into them."
I like how you never
underestimate my size.

Only now in shaded sunlight
do I see the reasons
for those questions.
I collected all of me and
pieced together a sky.
And as I open arms to
hold the world, I know.
Daddy,
I climb impossible mountains
because of you.

AFTER CAGES

Still new, and almost female
I remember doors closing,
backs turning, intuition
decisions made.
My body memorizing a prayer
it would recite again thirty years later:

> Hold on for mountains,
> they'll be rising.
> Hold on for rivers,
> they'll be running.
> Hold on for lessons,
> breaths and strokes . . .

Imagine you are history's cage.
Your body, a beautiful flesh-colored jail.
Your body wrapped tightly around
every ancestor's secret
like an heirloom quilt.
Keeping them tucked in, cherished, alive.
You are history's cage and your body is locked
around all that your ancestors moved for,
danced for, everything that made them sing and soar,

kill and crawl.
You have them all.
Behind your eyes,
under your tongue,
beneath your fingernails,
next to your heart like an extra rib.
One touch, carefully placed, sends them flying.
You are history's cage.
It is your job to keep them in.

> Hold on for seeds and softness.
> Hold on for windows and water.
> Hold on to the heavens with your breath.
> Hold on to the nest with your scream.
> You are your own mother.
> No one will ever love you more.

Learn to ride your memories
like a bird rides the sky.
Find the wind shifts,
let them lift you and turn you.
Roll the currents off your body
like the next word off your tongue.
Fly.
Welcome storms, sudden and serious.
Swim to the center.
Tread air.

History left you alone here,

don't let the future do the same.
Grab it by the shoulders,
cup its face, stroke its cheeks,
look it in the eyes and say, "Future, baby!
I thought I missed you. I thought
I'd have to spend the rest of my life without you."
Wink, flirt, kiss the future right on the lips
and don't be afraid to use a little tongue.

>Hold on for sunshine and shadows.
>Hold on to the earth with your feet.
>Hold on for nature to pick your heart,
>break the locks and send you airborne
>down the aisle bearing brilliant bouquets
>of fire and flowers.
>Hold on . . .

Because the future is flirting back.
Calling you by your name,
laughing at your jokes,
mooning about forever, forever . . .
and what do you think?
You think, "forever, forever . . ."
doesn't sound very carefree.
And you should know.

But the future is on one knee now
even while you are midair,
discovering aerodynamics

and learning to avoid cliffs when you soar.
And the future is stroking that spot
on the back of your neck,
whispering in your ear,
"Do you want me or not?"

But you are feeling the wind in your hair, finally
after all these years
and the answer is almost too easy:
Send history packing,
but keep the future panting.
Claim this sky for yourself.
Make it sacred.
Declare it off limits to anyone
who isn't madly in love with you.
Understand that not everyone will be.
But know that tomorrow will be waiting,
mouth open,
tongue extended
to taste you.

> Hold your breath for thirty years
> then break the surface slowly,
> skinless, liquid.
> You are your own lover.
> No one will ever love you more.

Amen.

MEMORY

for Angeline Salach

1.

There is a scream you are born with.
It hides in you like a secret
you promised God you would never tell.
It stays in you like a whisper
you only part your lips to
when love has left every other inch of you
as open as a wound.

There is a pain you are born with.
It aches in the furthest part of your heart.
It has no reason to leave.
It is warm and comfortable there,
inside you, waiting.

There is a peace you are born with.
You don't have to learn it.
It knows how to come and go from you
like a mother.
Like home.
Like breathing.

It is this breathing that has left me.
Replaced itself with some wild storm
and left me screaming for you:
the one who gave birth
to the one who gave birth to me.
My heart was built by you.
All bricks and breaths and beats and body.

The scream that kept itself hidden
has lifted the roof off my soul.
The one wrenching motion of air
that left you there, left me here.
Wishing I never made that promise to God.
Wishing the world would spin itself into reverse
so I could walk backwards with you
and play awhile.

The new breathing of pain comes
in waves, then in drops.
Wraps itself around us like skin,
sweating years and memories.
It is the room we go to cry in,
our bloodline leaving a trail
as red as the rose in your hand.
I've never seen red so cold,
so ice, so blue.
I wanted to follow you.
I wanted to hold your hand.
I wanted to never let go.

2.

When I heard you weren't here,
I heard the world crack open
and swallow me whole.

When I heard you weren't here,
I heard my heart gasp and break
into a hysterical new breathing
I couldn't catch up with.

When I heard you weren't here
I slipped into a new silence.
Strained my eyes to see in the dark.
Strained my ears to listen for memories.
When I heard you weren't here,
I heard the world crack open
and swallow me whole.

3.

Death brings with it a new vocabulary of time.
A sudden knowledge of how long *forever* is,
and everything I've always wanted to have,
and everything I've always wanted to be,
and every reason for moving becomes stilled
by one sudden heart-cracking, stomach-kicking,
I-never-expected-it-to-end
end.

And now,
starting anything
seems almost unfair.
Even beginning a sentence
feels like walking through mud.
Knee deep and over my head in thick wet earth,
I am grounded
and you are flying away.

I can only believe
how beautiful wings must feel
wrapped around your soul like a whisper.
Your new breathing comes in splashes,
then in rain.
Sweet and easy and forever.
Welcome home
singing softly in your ear.

I can only believe
how beautiful
that must feel.

MYTH

for Mark

This is the place I went to first,
grinning, giddy
with the truth.
My heart dark
red and open.
My birth imminent and over.

These are the opposites that cannot
attract if they do not know they
are not the same.
This is a happenstance
an unplanned victory
a strange and suspecting poignancy
the air refuses to let go of.
Big blue pushes of sky,
this is the roof over my head
this is the house I cannot live in alone
this is the decision I am not
responsible for right now
this is me being alive.

Can you tell the difference
from yesterday?
Did you notice the river is rising?
Do you remember the last time
that happened? I was fourteen.
I was eighteen. I was twenty-one.
Things were happening slower than I
would ever have believed

now
things were happening faster than I
could keep up with.
I was twenty-four.
Do you remember?
Something must have changed
on the Earth's face
at that moment:
a big sigh
a fragrant nod
to the gods who tend us
in their gardens
like their favorite flower.
Our disasters, weeds
to be potted as their plans.
This seed, they knew,
would grow tall.

Maybe they toasted each other,
glasses spilling over,

the rain this one time
leaving sweet sticky spots
all over our ground.
A gift for us.
Havens to crawl to
when we're starving,
and fly from
when we're full.

SPECIFICALLY

This is what I was afraid of:
This paper   this thought   lines
dividing white space   lines dividing
nothing.
This exhaustion   this futility
this game or promise.
                what dream
Your father
our baby
this apathy
this expanse of time
this thorn
sticking out of my
lips
keeping everyone
at talking distance.
This fire breathing
hard
singeing
tomorrow's crisp skirt.
This scab or
flower.

This water
glass
window
view of
      what dream
this ache
this loss
for words.

LOOKING FOR A SOFT PLACE TO LAND

for Zoe

1.

This is what I remember:
a crying inside from far away
sobbing
and my heart holding still enough
to hear itself breathe.
My ears, left with nothing to listen for
heard a sound   breaking
from far away.

I pushed you away and then
pulled you back and then pushed
you away and then pulled you back,
said goodbye a hundred times, said
I love you a hundred more, said
I love me most of all and
what do you think of that?
Caught myself
off guard   off balance
off to the side of the road
I told you to stay there, stay there,
until yesterday comes to find me.

Empty
full, lonely
far away
I wanted to be somewhere
with you, anywhere together
outside of me.
I've forgotten so much of what I started with.
Could I make a deal with you maybe
rearrange a few chromosones
walk backwards leap forwards name you now
and recognize you later?
If I let you go will you come back
will you forgive me will you be mine?
Tell me.
There's a handprint on my heart.
I didn't think it would be so hard
to say good-bye
before we even said hello.

2.

This love is a wish
made before you were born.
Of all the things you don't want
to have to ask for.
Of all the things you'll need
to keep breathing.
If you could send a message ahead,

let them know what's on your mind,
even though you haven't stepped
a foot outside the womb
you've got some ideas,
some desires some demands:
Let it be warm let it be soft let it be true.

Are you my family?
Birth begins and with this first breath
eyes closed mouth open wide screaming
to the world, *are you my family?*
Who's gonna be my family?
Look down at one cord connecting you
to one body your first home suddenly
miles away, *what does this mean?*
Are you my family?

3.

This love is a hurricane
tornado twisting touching down on you
wrapping you up in its vertigo violence
leaving history in its wake, its dust
drenched with remembering.
This love is gusty winds howling
at midnight changing seasons midbreath,
blowing hot and cold
through the draftiest parts

of your family
asking *are you gonna fix this house?*
Who's gonna fix this house?

Who's gonna bring the hammer
down on the first promise, pounding
what was into what should've been.
Who will bring the water?
Who will love this house, tend it
like a garden, nurture it
like a mother a father a friend
a stranger passing by
who just had to stop and ask:
Are you gonna fix this house?
Who's gonna fix this house?

4.

This is us: blindfolded
and full of faith.
Being spun around and around until
nothing is where you remember
it being before.
Until nothing is still.
Walking forward
to pin the tail on the donkey
and missing by a mile.

5.

We've all had to choose something
we didn't want to not want so
what was your choice?
Your moment of memory screaming
back at you: BAIL OUT!
BAIL OUT NOW! Go backwards leap
forwards do what you have to
but save yourself!
History is an excellent writer
so don't you worry about having to
give it any ideas just BAIL OUT!
HEAD FOR THE FUTURE!
Don't look behind you and don't stop now
because what's followingthisclose is
an army of alternatives, every choice
you never made, every other in your past
that never became your future, every
thing that made a difference
by never being born, BAIL OUT!
Run far and run forward
on legs that have grown strong
outpacing what will never be, RUN!
Run until you can't run anymore
run until you can't run anymore
run until you have to

J
 U
M
 P
 !

6.

You hear two hearts beating
and only one of them is yours.
You are floating now, in water
or air, it doesn't matter.
One of them is holding you up.
It is the world as you know it:
warm, soft, true.
Just this once you want memory
to be able to leap ahead of you,
catch the future,
save it for the past.

7.

Home.
The older you are,
the harder it is to find.
The farther you have to fall
after you jump.
And you have jumped.

You are drifting down now
like Dorothy, looking for a soft place,
or an evil witch, to land on.
You are drifting down and someone shouts
T H I S   I S   Y O U R   L I F E . . .
and history reels by you like strips
of film from a feature length movie.
So many frames per second
so many frames per memory
so many frames per home.

Are you my family?
The question leaps from your mouth,
a brave skydiver jumping ahead to
find an answer and have it waiting
when you touch the ground.
An anxious air traffic controller guiding you
carefully, your fleshy plane suddenly
aching to land:

> A little more to the left, right, left
> bring her down slowly, slowly.
> O.K., we've got you on radar now.

Are you my family?

Yes. The answer
ripples out from the ground like
echoes from a million mountain tops.
Like water from a single drop.

Yes. And it comes to you like a choir.
Brave harmonies rise to meet you and
your mouth, crowded with emotion,
can only listen and believe.
It is the world groaning back at you
giving birth even as we speak.
Truth has built a nest here.

Are you my family?
Yes, I am.
We are.
You land.
It is soft.

WIRELESS BALLROOM

Translations swim through the sea,
wash up on my beach,
flop on my sand and
beg to be heard.
Words with no country
to call them home.
Words with no voice
to clothe their edges.
Our conversation follows
a map of a world well-versed
in universal manners.
We are global.
History cannot touch us.
We are the future.

Scrambled voices
find each other in some
wireless ballroom, off some
super highway, dangle
gracefully without a net
three hundred feet below sea level.

Scrambled voices
find each other in less
than the second it takes
to speak *hello* out loud.

We do not need proof that this
is an improvement over flesh.
Flesh can break, tear, rip, bleed.
Flesh wounds too easily
and takes too long to fix.
It cannot carry us where we want to go.

Our new future will come fast
and furious with the past
for taking so damn long
to get us here.

The Ocean's Reply

Lay your wires under me
stretch your industrial imaginations
across my sea.
You have claimed the right
to talk to tomorrow.
If I tell you you haven't,
you will breathe war.

Lay your wires under me
open your mouths and send their contents
spilling across my unmade bed.
Words sprouting underwater wings,
learning to breathe with gills,
growing scales.
Words learning to swim.
Avoiding baited hooks,
baited countries,
holding their messages in like air,
heroically refusing to exhale
until they have reached the opposite shore.

You are my opposite shore.

I hear you but I cannot feel you.
I hold you but I cannot touch you.
Inside your skin, nerves bristle
with unused responses anxious to react.
Inside your skin, bones float and fall
anxious to dance a holier dance.
Inside your skin, conversations
swirl and sputter.
Nervy sentences work their way
to your fingertips.
Your mouth has already forgotten
what to do in this situation.
You have ten tongues to make your point.
Ears fall like rain.
You listen with your eyes
and nod and type back YES I'M HERE.

What do you want to tell me,
what do you want me to know?
Wrinkled maps grace your skin,
pointing me to every place you've ever been.
The hearts you've taken residence in.
The homes you've built with your own.
Flesh cannot lie.
Time will trace you with true stories
that can never be smoothed or stitched
or simply deleted from your skin.
Flesh is forever fallible.
It will give you away every time.

Open pores spilling secrets, chattering
constantly, gasping and gossiping,
new cells, new life, new muscle.

What do I want you to know?
This body.
This body of information.
This body of information must be
confronted and caressed and conversed with.
This body of information cannot be
foldered and filed and called up on command.
This body of information is not easily accessible.
Dance with me and you'll know.

Flesh can send a scientist screaming
or drive an inventor insane.
Like the ocean it swam out of,
it was divinely designed.
Proficient. Potent. Waterproof.
Like the heart it encloses,
it must be prayed for and prodded,
bullied and babied and eventually, buried.

But the fingerprints it leaves behind,
the layers of lifetimes,
every relationship's ripple,
will continue to spurt and spawn
new skin. New stories.
Human handholds for the future.

AFTER BIRTH

This is not a clean place.
There are not drawers
to fit everything.
Sometimes the rubbish
piles up so high, it is
taller than me.
It could be a forest.
Damp smelling.
An odor of things fertilizing
other things,
making each other grow.
Not to be generous
or even polite
but because that is the nature
of nature. Everything
on purpose, nothing from spite.
There is really only one
reason for doing anything:
To be born, and reborn,
and live in between
the deaths.

About the Author

CIN SALACH has been performing her words around the country since 1987. A member of the first National Slam Championship team, she was chosen to be Chicago's cultural ambassador to Prague, Czech Republic, in 1989. A participant since 1990 in the women's performance extravaganza, *Big Goddess Pow Wow*, Cin is also the co-founder of the Loofah Method and Betty's Mouth—two poetic, duetic, multi-mediatic performance groups. Her CD and video recordings with both have been seen and heard on WBEZ, *Studs Terkel Show, Image Union*, and *Oprah!* This is her first printed experience.